CHILDREN'S LIBRARY

THE LIBERTY BELL

Joe Gaspar

PowerKiDS
press™

New York

Published in 2014 by The Rosen Publishing Group, Inc.
29 East 21st Street, New York, NY 10010

Copyright © 2014 by The Rosen Publishing Group, Inc.

First Edition

Editor: Amelie von Zumbusch
Book Design: Colleen Bialecki

Photo Credits: Cover Racheal Grazias/Shutterstock.com; p. 5 DC Productions/Photodisc/Thinkstock; pp. 7, 13, 17 Superstock/Getty Images; pp. 9, 15, 21 Visions of America/Universal Images Group/Getty Images; p. 11 Mark Krapels/Shutterstock.com; p. 19 Spirit of America/Shutterstock.com; p. 23 Don Murray/Getty Images News/Getty Images; p. 24 idea for life/Shutterstock.com.

Library of Congress Cataloging-in-Publication Data

Gaspar, Joe.
  The Liberty Bell / by Joe Gaspar. — First edition.
      pages cm. — (Powerkids readers: American symbols)
  Includes index.
  ISBN 978-1-4777-0739-5 (library binding) — ISBN 978-1-4777-0819-4 (pbk.) —
  ISBN 978-1-4777-0820-0 (6-pack)
  1. Liberty Bell—Juvenile literature. 2. Philadelphia (Pa.)—Buildings, structures, etc.—Juvenile literature. I. Title.
  F158.8.I3G37 2014
  974.8'11—dc23
                          2012046181

Manufactured in the United States of America

CPSIA Compliance Information: Batch #S13PK4: For Further Information contact Rosen Publishing, New York, New York at 1-800-237-9932

CONTENTS

The Liberty Bell....................4

Liberty Bell History..............12

Visiting the Bell.................. 22

Words to Know.................. 24

Index.................................. 24

Websites............................24

This is the **Liberty Bell**.

It is old.

PROCLAIM LIBERTY

PASS AND STOW
PHILAD^A
MDCCLIII

7

It is big.

9

It is in Philadelphia, Pennsylvania.

It was made in England.

It is mostly **copper**.

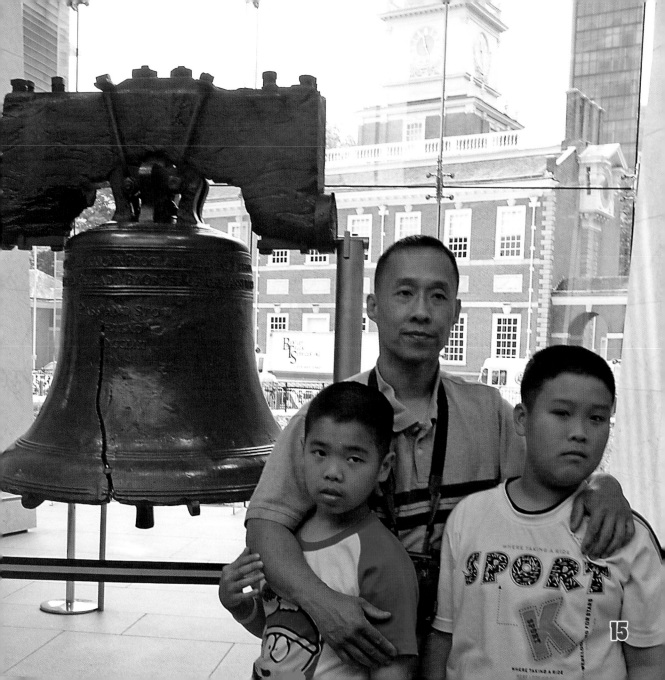

Its old name is the State House Bell.

It has a **crack**.

It is rung two days a year.

21

You can visit it.

WORDS TO KNOW

copper

crack

Liberty Bell

INDEX

C
copper, 14
crack, 18

E
England, 12

N
name, 16

P
Philadelphia,
Pennsylvania, 10

WEBSITES

Due to the changing nature of Internet links, PowerKids Press has developed an online list of websites related to the subject of this book. This site is updated regularly. Please use this link to access the list: www.powerkidslinks.com/pkras/bell/